The teachings

AMINAH BRENDA LYNN ROBINSON

The Teachings

Drawn from African-American Spirituals

Harcourt Brace Jovanovich, Publishers

New York   San Diego   London

Requests for permission to make copies of any part of the
work should be mailed to: Permissions Department,
Harcourt Brace Jovanovich, Publishers, 8th Floor,
Orlando, Florida 32887.

Library of Congress Cataloging-in-Publication Data
Robinson, Aminah Brenda Lynn.
The teachings: drawn from African-American
spirituals/by Aminah Brenda Lynn Robinson.—1st ed.
p.   cm.
ISBN 0-15-188126-X
ISBN 0-15-688247-7 (pbk.)
1. Robinson, Aminah Brenda Lynn. 2. Spirituals (Songs)—
Illustrations.   I. Title.
NC975.5.R58A4   1992
741.973—dc20   92-18614

First edition   A B C D E

The illustrations in this book
were done in pen and ink on typewriter paper.
The display type and text type were set in Simoncini Garamond
by HBJ Photocomposition Center, San Diego, California.
Color separations by Bright Arts, Ltd., Singapore
Printed by The Eusey Press, Inc., Leominster, Massachusetts
Bound by Book Press, Inc., Brattleboro, Vermont
Production supervision by Warren Wallerstein and David Hough
Designed by Camilla Filancia

To my parents, my first teachers,
LEROY WILLIAM EDWARD ROBINSON *and*
HELEN ELIZABETH ZIMMERMAN ROBINSON,
and to MRS. URSEL MAXINE WHITE LEWIS,
mentor, teacher, and lifelong friend,
who led me deep into the life, culture,
and history of African-American people

CONTENTS

Memories, woven together like the threads
of treasured family cloths, are protected
and loved through generations; the sharing
of memories becomes the story of all of our
lives. Over time, memories become our history, telling us who we have been and who
we are becoming. African-American slaves
created such stories of themselves in the
spirituals.

"The teachings," my interpretations of
the spirituals, are created from the words
and images that come to me through these
memories. They have grown from the
stories and songs that were given to me by

my family and my early teachers, and I offer them here to the children of today's troubled world and the children of tomorrow. They carry a message of dignity, knowledge, and wisdom. Through the teachings of the past, young people will know that they can reach their aspirations, can develop the beauty that is within them, and can sing praises in freedom and confidence.

The spirituals speak of survival, of freedom and determination, of love and faith, of justice and of hope. The spirituals, weaving together the memories that carry us into the future, must not be forgotten. They are our stories, our chants, our dreams, our lives. As they did so long ago, they continue to reach out and offer hope.

—Aminah Brenda Lynn Robinson
Columbus, Ohio
June 1992

The Teachings

KEEP YOUR EYES ON THE PRIZE

Keep your eyes on the prize—

You better run, 'fore the train done gone!

Keep your eyes on the prize,

Keep your hand upon the chariot,

For the preacher's comin'

An' he preach so bold of salvation from out of his soul—

Oh, keep your hand upon the chariot

And your eyes on the prize . . .

KEEP YOUR EYES ON THE PRIZE

Keep your eyes on the prize—
u better run, 'fore the brain
me gone! Keep your eyes on the prize,
keep your hand upon the chariot,
for the preacher's comin' an' he
reach so bold of salvation from
it of his Soul —— Oh, keep
our hand upon the chariot
and your eyes on the prize...

HOLD ON!

Keep yo' hand on de plow,

Hold on! Hold on!

Mother, Mother, let me come in—

Door's all fastened an' de windows pinned—

Keep yo' hand on de plow,

Hold on!

Father said, Ya lost yo' track,

Can' plow straight an' keep a-lookin' back—

Hold on!

Sisters, Hold on!

Brothers, Hold on!

Children, Hold on!

Keep your han' on de gospel plow!

Hold on!

Keep your han' on dat great plow, an'

Hold on!

keep yo' hand on de plow,
hold on! Hold on!
Mother, mother, let me
come in— door's all
dstned an' de windows
pinned— keep yo' hand
n de plow, Hold on!
'ather said, ya lost
yo' track, can' plow
staight an' keep a-
lookin' back— Hold on!
Sisters, Hold on!
Brothers, Hold on!
Children, Hold on!
keep your han'
on de gosple
plow!
  Hold on!
keep your
han' on dat
great plow,
an'
  Hold
  on!

HOLD ON!

WOKE UP THIS MORNIN'
WITH MY MIN' ON FREEDOM

Woke up this mornin' with my min' on freedom

An' it was stayed—

Can't hate your neighbor in your min',

If you keep it stayed,

De devil can't catch you in your min',

If you keep it stayed,

Jesus is de Captain in your min',

When you keep it stayed . . .

16

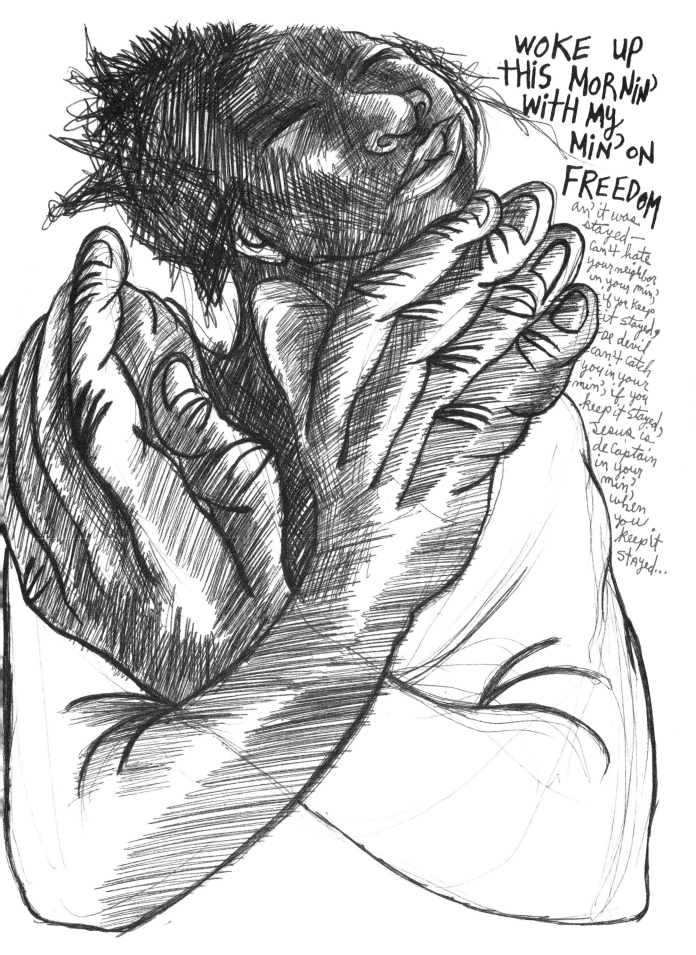

WOKE UP
THIS MORNIN'
WITH MY
MIN' ON
FREEDOM
an' it was
stayed—
can't hate
your neighbor
in your min',
if you keep
it stayed,
de devil
can't catch
you in your
min', if you
keep it stayed,
Jesus is
de Captain
in your
min',
when
you
keep it
stayed...

WEEPING MARY

If there's anybody here like weeping Mary—

Call upon your Jesus and He'll draw near—

Weepin' Mary, weepin' Mary—

You need not always weep and moan,

And wear these slavery chains forlorn!

If there's anybody here like weeping Mary—

Call upon your Jesus and He'll draw near. . . .

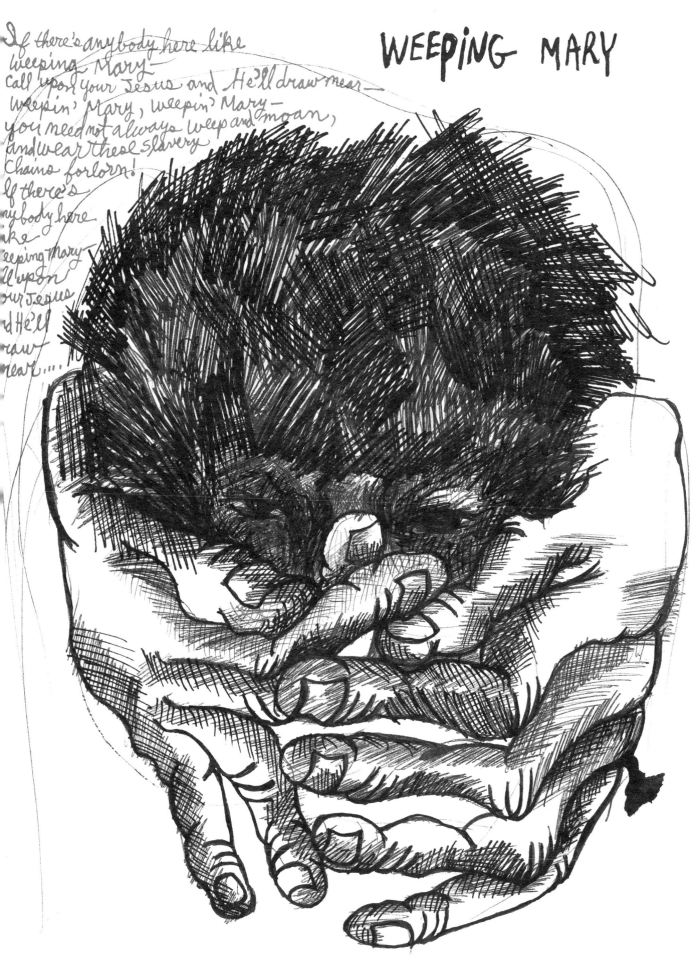

WEEPING MARY

If there's anybody here like
weeping Mary—
call upon your Jesus and He'll draw near—
weepin' Mary, weepin' Mary—
you need not always weep and moan,
and wear these slavery
chains forlorn!
If there's
nybody here
ike
eeping Mary—
ll upon
ur Jesus
d He'll
raw
near....

SCANDALIZE' MY NAME

Well, I met my sister de other day,

Give her my right han',

Jesus, as soon as ever my back was turned

She took 'n' scandalize' my name.

Do you call dat a sister?

No! No!—

Scandalize' my name!

SCANDALIZE? MY NAME

ell, I met my Sister de other Day,
'ive her my right han', Jesus, as
oon as 'ever my Back was turned
he took 'n' scandalize' my name.
—you call dat a Sister? No! No!—
Scandalize' my name!

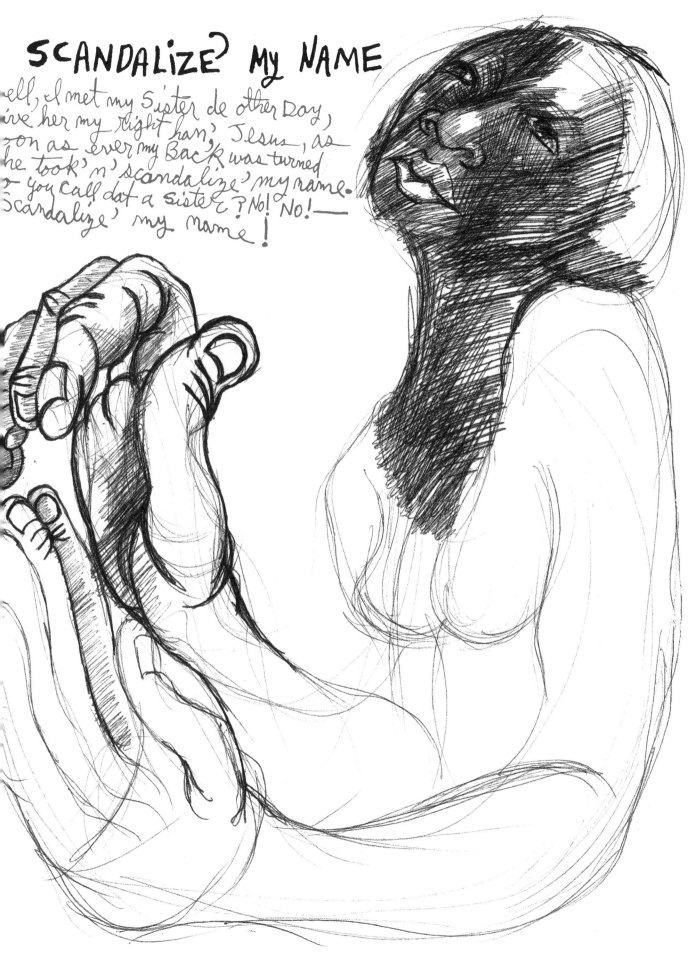

DEEP RIVER

.

Deep River,

My home is over Jordan—

I want to cross over into Campground.

O don't you want to go to that gospel feast,

That Promisland where all is peace?

Oh!

DEEP RIVER

DeepRiver, My home
is over Jordan—
I want to cross
over into Campground.
O don't you want to
go to that gospel
feast, that
Promisland
where all is
Peace? oh!

GIVE ME JESUS

I heard my mother say,

Give me Jesus.

Dark midnight was my cry,

Give me Jesus—

You may have all this world—

Give me Jesus!

24

GIVE ME JESUS

I heard my Mother say,
Give me Jesus.
Dark midnight was my cry,
Give me Jesus—
You may have all this world—
Give me Jesus!

MY LORD, WHAT A MORNING

My Lord, what a morning!

When the stars begin to fall.

You will hear the trumpet sound—

To wake the nations underground,

Standin' at my God's right hand,

When the stars begin to fall.

26

My Lord
what a morning!
when the stars begin
to fall. You will
hear the trumpet sound
to wake the nations
underground, standing
at my my God's right hand,
when the stars begin to fall.

MY LORD,
WHAT A MORNING

WE SHALL OVERCOME

We shall overcome,

We shall overcome someday;

If in our hearts we do believe,

We shall overcome someday.

We'll walk hand in hand;

We shall all have peace,

We are not afraid;

God is not through with us yet . . .

We shall overcome someday,

Oh, if in our hearts we do believe,

We shall overcome someday!

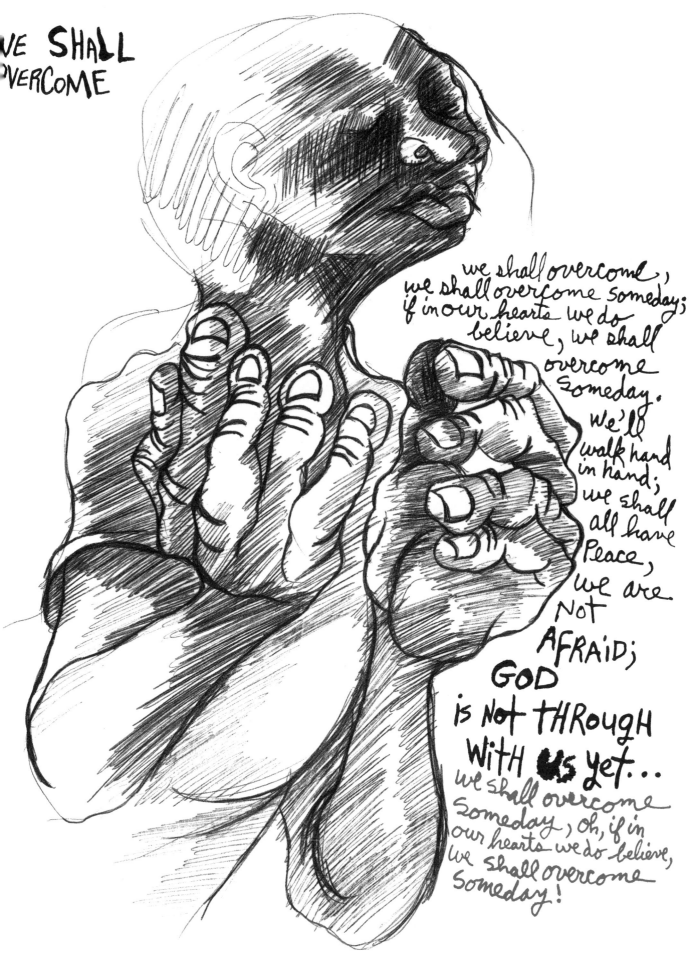

I'LL TAKE THE WINGS OF THE MORNING

I'll take the wings of the morning

And now let me fly!

Way down yonder in de middle o' de fiel',

Angel workin' at de chariot wheel,

Not so good 'bout workin' at de wheel,

I jes' want to see how de chariot feel—

I'll take the wings of the morning—

Now let me fly!

Meet dat hypocrite on de street,

First thing she do is to show her teeth.

Nex' thing she do is to tell a lie,

An' de bes' thing to do is to pass her by!

I'll take the wings of the morning—

Now let me fly!

Let me fly!

I'LL TAKE THE
WINGS OF THE
MORNING

and, now let me fly!
y down yonder in de middle o' de fiel',
gel workin' at de
riot wheel,
 so good
out workin'
de wheel,
yu' want
see how
Chariot
feel—
I'll take
he wings
f the
morning—
ow let
me fly!
neet dat
hypocrite
on de street,
first thing
she do is
to show
her teeth.
ney' thing
she do is
to tell
a lie,
an' de
bes' thing
to do is to
Pass her by!
I'll take the wings
of the morning—
Now let me fly!
Let me fly!

MOTHERLESS CHILD

Sometimes I feel like a motherless child,

A long ways from home—

True believer, a long ways from home.

Sometimes I feel like I'm almos' gone,

A long ways from home.

Then I get down on my knees an' pray—

Way up in the heavenly land home

A long ways from home.

MOTHERLESS CHILD

Sometimes I feel like a Motherless Child,
A long ways from home—
True believer, a long ways from
home. Sometimes I feel like I'm
almos' gone, a long ways from
home. Then I get down on my
knees an' pray—
way up in the
heavenly land home.
A long ways from home.

I'VE BEEN 'BUKED

I've been 'buked an'

I've been scorned,

I've been talked about

Sho's you' born.

Dere is trouble all over dis worl'—

Ain' gwine lay my 'ligion down . . .

I've Been 'BUKED

I've been 'buked an'
I've been scorned,
I've been talked about
sho's you' born.
Dere is trouble all over dis worl'
I ain' gwine lay my 'ligion down...

SWING LOW,
SWEET CHARIOT

Swing low, sweet chariot,

Coming for to carry me home—

I look over Jordan,

And what did I see,

A band of angels—

If you get there before I do,

Tell all my friends—

I'm sometimes up,

I'm sometimes down,

But still my soul feels—

Coming for to carry me home . . .

SWING LOW,
SWEET CHARIOT

Swing low, sweet chariot,
coming for to carry me home — I look
over Jordan, and what did I see, a
band of angels — if you get there before
I do, tell all my friends — I'm
sometimes up, I'm sometimes
down, but still my soul feels
coming for to carry me home...

I GOT A KEY
TO THAT KINGDOM

O get your trumpet Gabriel and come down on the sea.

Now don't you sound your trumpet till you get orders from me—

I got a key to that Kingdom!

And the world can't do me no harm!

Gabriel, Gabriel, blow your trumpet!

My Lord says he's going to rain down fire.

Oh, He's going to wake up the dead, going to wake up the dead—

One of these mornings bright and fair,

God's going to wake up the dead—

I got a key to that Kingdom!

I GOT A KEY TO THAT KINGDOM

O get your trumpet Gabriel
and come down on the sea. Now
don't you sound your trumpet
till you get orders from me—
I got a key to that kingdom!
And the world can't do me no harm!
Gabriel, Gabriel, blow your
trumpet! My Lord says
he's going to rain down fire.
Oh, he's going to wake
up the dead, going to
wake up the dead—
One of these mornings
bright and fair,
God's going to wake
up the dead—
I got a key
to that kingdom!

AMAZING GRACE

Amazing grace,

How sweet the sound,

That saved a wretch like me!

I once was lost, but now I'm found,

Was blind, but now I see.

Grace that taught my heart to fear,

And grace my fears relieved;

How precious did that grace appear,

The hour I first believed!

When we've been there ten thousand years,

Bright shining as the sun,

We've no less days to sing God's praise

Than when we'd first begun.

Many dangers, toils, and snares,

I have already come;

'Twas grace that brought me safe thus far,

And grace will lead me home!

AMAZING GRACE

how sweet the sound,
that saved a wretch
like me! I once was
lost, but now I'm
found, was blind,
but now I see.
Grace that taught my
heart to fear, and Grace
my fears relieved;
How precious did
that grace appear
the hour I first
believe!
When we've been there
ten thousand years,
Bright Shining as the Sun,
we've no less days to sing
God's Praise—
Then when we'd
first begun.

Many dangers,
toils, and snares,
I have already
come; 'twas grace
that brought me
safe this far,
and grace will
lead me home!

BE STILL AND KNOW
FOR HE NEVUH SAID
A MUMBALIN' WORD

Be still and know!

He never said a mumbalin' word.

They nailed Him to the tree,

And they pierced Him in the side,

And the blood came streamin' down—

He never said a mumbalin' word

As He hung His head and died—

Be still and know,

For He never said a mumbalin' word,

Not a word, not a word, not a word—

Be still and know!

Be still and know! He never said a mumbalin' word.
They nailed Him to the tree, and they pierced
Him in the side, and the blood came
streamin' down— He never
said a mumbalin' word as He
hung His head and died—
   Be Still and Know, for He never
said a mumbalin'
word, not a
word, not a word,
Not a word—
e Still and
Know!

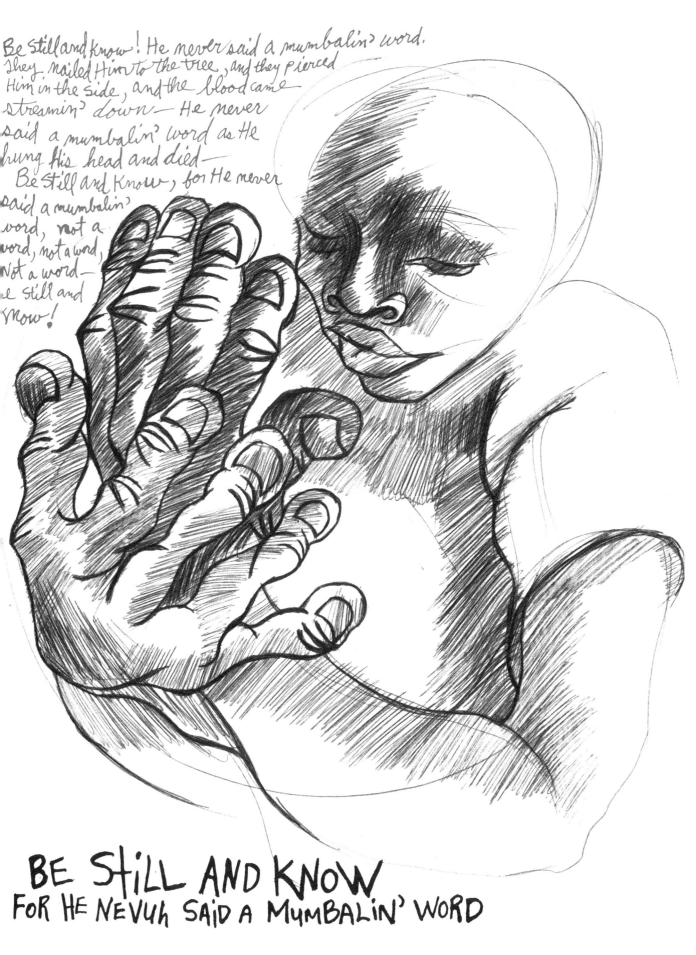

BE STILL AND KNOW
FOR HE NEVUH SAID A MUMBALIN' WORD

FREE AT LAST

I's free, I's free, I's free at las'!

Thank God A'mighty, I's free at las'!

Surely been 'buked, and surely been scorned,

Still my soul is heaven born!

If you don't know that I been redeemed,

Follow me down to Jordan's stream,

Free at last!

Thank God A'mighty, I's free at las'!

44

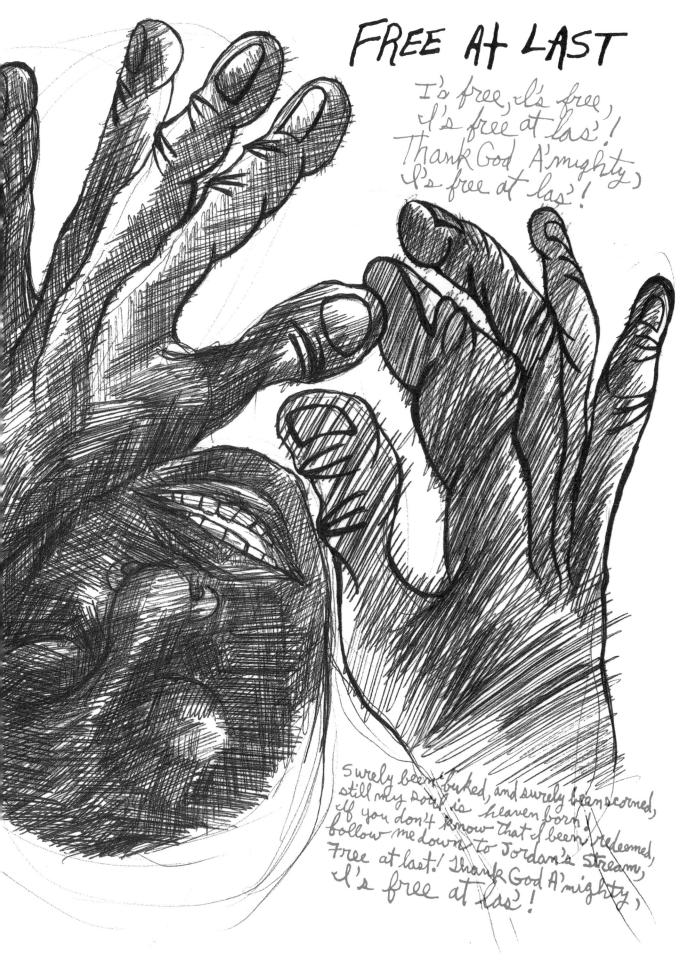

FREE At LAST

I's free, I's free,
I's free at las'!
Thank God A'mighty,
I's free at las'!

Surely been 'buked, and surely been scorned,
Still my soul is heaven born,
If you don't know that I been redeemed,
follow me down to Jordan's stream,
Free at last! Thank God A'mighty,
I's free at las'!

GO DOWN, MOSES

When Israel was in Egypt's land—

Let my people go—

Oppressed so hard they could not stand,

Let my people go—

Go down, Moses, 'way down in Egyptland,

Tell ole Pharaoh, let my people go.

No more shall they in bondage toil—

Let them come out with Egypt's spoil—

The Lord told Moses what to do—

To lead the children of Israel through—

O come along, Moses, you'll not get lost,

Stretch out your rod and come across—

Oh, Moses, the cloud shall clear the way—

A fire by night, a shade by day . . .

We need not always weep and moan—

And wear these slavery chains forlorn . . .

GO DOWN, MOSES

when Israel was in Egypt's land—
Let my people go — oppressed so
hard they could not stand, Let my
people go — Go down, Moses, 'way
down in Egypt land, Tell de Pharaoh,
Let my people go. No more shall they,
in bondage toil— Let them come out with
Egypt's Spoil — The Lord told Moses
what to do— to lead the children of
Israel through — O come along, Moses,
you'll not get lost, stretch out your rod
and come across — Oh, Moses, the
cloud shall clear the way — A fire by
night, a Shade by Day.....

We need not always weep
and moan — and wear
these slavery
chains
forlorn...

No more auction block for me,

No more! No more!

No more peck o' corn for me,

No more! No more!

No more driver's lash for me,

No more! No more!

No more hundred lash for me,

No more! No more!

I take my freedom to the river of Jordan,

Many thousand gone—many thousand gone.

No more lynchings in my backyard!

No more Auschwitzs and Belsens in this world tomorrow!

No more, no more!

Many thousand gone—

No more bombings, no more riots,

No more drugs in our communities today!

Many thousand gone.

I take my freedom to the midnight sun!

Many thousand gone.

MANY
THOUSAND
GONE

No more Auction
Block for me,
No more! No more!
No more Peck o' corn
for me, No more! No more!
No more driver's lash
for me, No more! No More!
No more hundred lash
for me, No More! No more!
Take my Freedom
to the River of Jordan,
Many thousand GONE—
Many thousand GONE.
No more lynchings in my backyard!
No more Auschwitz's and Belsen's in this world tomorrow!
No more, No more! Many thousand Gone—
No more bombings, no more riots, no more Drugs in
our Communities today! Many thousand gone.
Take my freedom to the Midnight sun!
Many thousand Gone.

NOBODY KNOWS DE TROUBLE I'VE SEEN

Nobody knows the trouble I've seen—

Nobody knows but Jesus.

Sometimes I'm up, sometimes I'm down,

Sometimes I'm almost to the ground . . .

Sisters, will you pray for me.

Mothers, will you pray for me . . .

NoBody Knows de
Trouble I've seen

Body knows the trouble I've seen—
obody knows but Jesus.
Sometimes I'm up, sometimes I'm
down, Sometimes I'm almost to
e ground....
Sisters will you pray for me.
Mothers,
ill you pray
a me....

J U B I L E E

Jubilee, O Lordy—

What is the matter, the Church won't shout?

What is the matter with the mourner?

O—what is the matter, the Church won't move?

Somebody in there that ought-a be out!

The devil's in the Amen corner!

My Lord, Jubilee!

Somebody in there that's carryin' bad news!

52

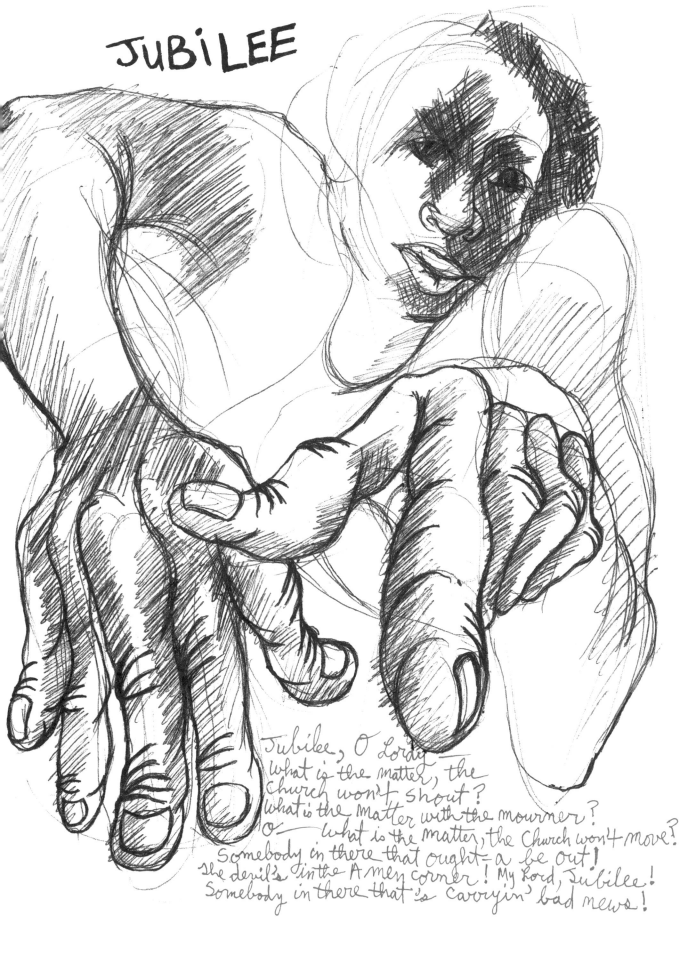

JUBILEE

Jubilee, O Lord,
What is the matter, the
Church won't shout?
What is the matter with the mourner?
O— what is the matter, the Church won't move?
Somebody in there that ought-a be out!
The devil's in the Amen corner! My Lord, Jubilee!
Somebody in there that's carryin' bad news!

WHAT YOU GONNA NAME THAT PRETTY LITTLE BABY?

Oh, Mary, what you gonna name that pretty little Baby?

Glory, Glory to the newborn King!

Some will call Him one thing, but I think I'll call him Jesus!

Glory, Glory, Glory, Glory to the newborn King!

54

WHAT you
gonna Name
THAT pretty
Little Baby?

Oh, Mary, what you gonna
name that pretty
little Baby? Glory, Glory
to the new born King!
Some will call Him one
thing, but I think I'll
call Him Jesus! Glory,
Glory, Glory
to the new born King!

DOWN ON HUH, DOWN ON HUH!

I don't know what my mother wants to stay here fuh,

Dis ole worl' ain't been no friend to huh—

Sometimes she's up, sometimes she's down,

Sometimes she's almost on the ground.

Looks like everybody in the whole round world

Is down on huh, down on huh.

I don't know what my mother wants to stay here fuh,

Dis ole worl' ain't been no friend to huh!

LET US CROSS OBER DE RIVER

O Lawd, ain't dey rest fo' de weary one?

One star in the east, one star in de west—

And I wish dat star was in mah breast!

Let us cross ober de ribber an' rest.

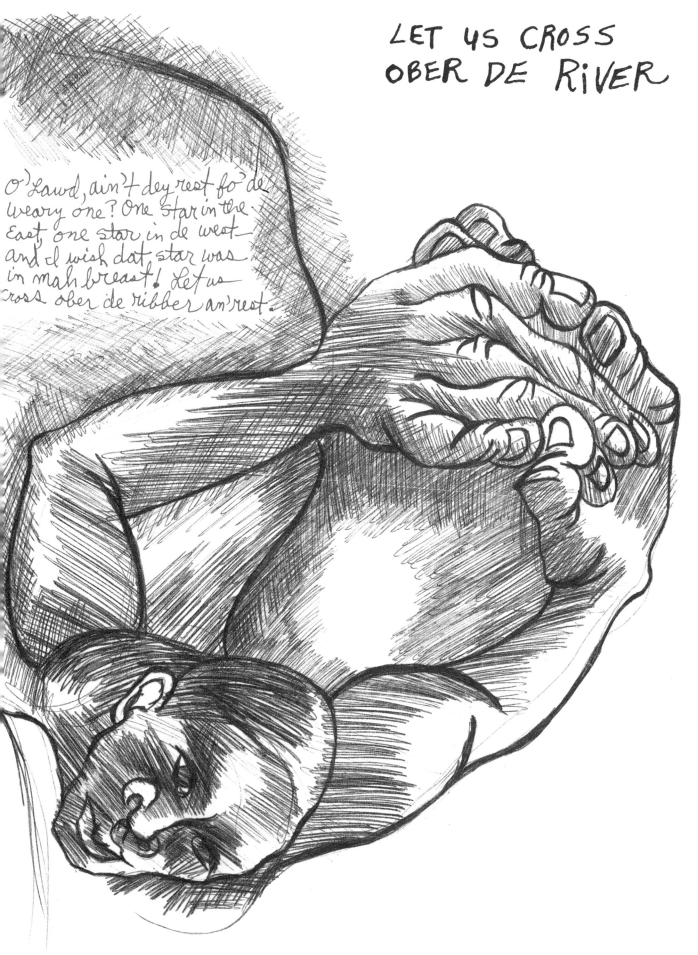

LET US CROSS
OBER DE RIVER

O' Lawd, ain't dey rest fo' de
weary one? One star in the
East, one star in de west
and I wish dat star was
in mah breast! Let us
cross ober de ribber an' rest.

STEAL AWAY

Steal away, steal away to Jesus!

Steal away home, I ain't got long to stay here!

My Lord calls me,

He calls me by the thunder,

The trumpet sounds within a my soul,

I ain't got long to stay here.

Steal away home to Jesus. . . .

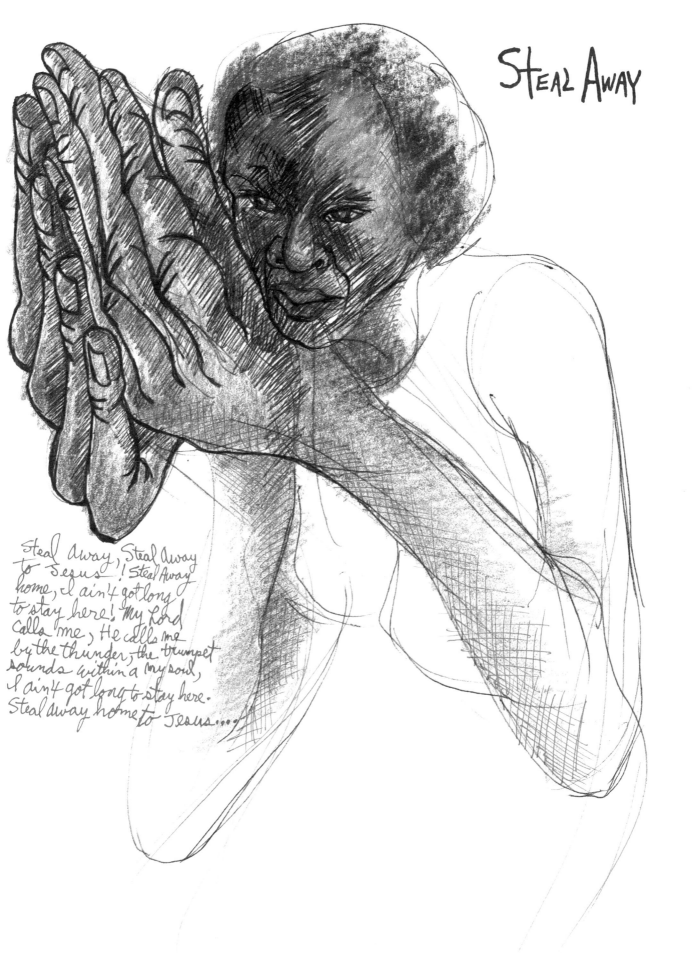

Steal Away

Steal Away, Steal Away
to Jesus! Steal Away
home, I ain't got long
to stay here! My Lord
calls me, He calls me
by the thunder, the trumpet
sounds within a my soul,
I ain't got long to stay here.
Steal away home to Jesus....

PRAISES TO GOD

On mah journey now,

Well I wouldn't take nothin' for mah journey now!

Praises to God—

One day I was walking along,

Well the elements opened an' de love come down—

Praises to God!

I went to de valley an' I didn't go to stay,

Well, my soul got happy an' I stayed all day!

Praises to God!

Praises to God!

PRAISES TO GOD

On mah journey now,
well I wouldn't take
nothin' for mah
journey now!
Praises to God—
ne day I was walking
long, well the elements
ened an' de love come
own— Praises to God!

I went to de valley
an' I didn't go
to stay,
well, my
soul got
happy
an' I
stayed
all
day!
Praises
to
God!
Praises
to
God!